MW00572254

DISCOURSE 007

Uneasy Listening:
Notes on Hearing
and Being Heard

Anouchka Grose &
Robert Brewer Young

'What do you think the sounds of an organ come out of? Or the sounds of a violin or even of a whistle? The fact is that by using a mechanical contrivance, a violinist or an organist can express something poignantly human that cannot be expressed without the mechanical contrivance. To achieve such an expression of course the violinist or organist has to have interiorized the technology, made the tool or machine a second nature, a psychological part of him or herself.'
– Walter J. Ong, *Orality and Literacy*

For a while I had been wondering what it might be possible to say about listening. Either it's a total non-subject, or it's the most important activity in the world. In my work as a psychoanalyst, I sometimes find myself sitting there thinking, 'Let's be honest, this isn't really a thing, is it?' But then again I think, 'Oh yes it is. What if no one ever listened to you? That would be terrible. Just because I can't directly provide this person with money/love/interesting work it doesn't follow that I am useless.'

I also know from the limited amount of climate activism I do that people who live in places that are currently burning, melting, or flooding are anxious to be heard. They will often say things like, 'We need the rest of the world to listen. We're not just trying to save ourselves, we're trying to save you too.' Wealthy, post-industrial societies are built on the premise of non-listening. If we actually listened to the people we were screwing over we would surely do something about exploitation, enforced labour, debt, and environmental destruction.

Listening promises to open up the possibility of both speaker and hearer being transformed. But how? I had the idea that if I tried to write about it, I'd at the very least reinvigorate my clinical work and at most save the planet and bring about world peace.

As it goes with these things, having had the idea I then had to write an outline – part boast, part promise – detailing what I intended to say. As soon as you've designated a topic as interesting it either instantly drains of all interest or becomes so complex and impossible that you no longer know what to say about it. What you do at this point is to jot down something provisional in the hope that the real ideas will come later.

I had dashed off an outline and was happily getting on with not writing anything when I became aware of a violin-maker and philosopher called Robert Brewer Young. I was curious about the kind of listening that might be involved in making, or mending, a musical instrument. I imagined the nature of the listening he specialised in must be very different from mine. I hoped I could learn a great deal from him, and that this would morph into the 'real' ideas I'd been waiting for. His seemed a kind of super-listening, like that of a highly cultured bat or wolf, whereas mine was more chatty. Still, I was concerned at the prospect of vampirising Robert's thoughts. Plus it was difficult to arrange to vampirise him as we were in lockdown, and he had just broken his leg. Instead, I wrote him a letter asking if he would like to work on a very small book with me and, fortunately, he replied and said yes.

The approximation of perfect sense is what we can hope for when speaking, but can there be a higher bar, a better target, something we might risk calling 'true' when we are listening? 'Thoughts die when embodied in words.' Schopenhauer's old harangue against the attempt at anything – in language at least – that tries to render the landscape of the imagination and its damned and yet sometimes bright and clear instants. In the moment before opening our mouths, is there a potential, or process of attunement, to attend to?

I spend my life and make my living listening, working for blistered hours on end to give cuts of wood something to say by making them into instruments. The language to describe the solitary encounter with the select slab of a tree eludes me, but I have to start listening early on, to how wet it is on a saw, how quickly sound dies within it when rapped with a knuckle, how brittle it may be when run through with a small plane. When it has strings pulled over it months later and a musician comes to my aid – and maybe I to theirs – our task is to listen and drive something into language that tells us how to temper and tame things.

Fortunately the last word is music, which we know can't be pinned down even by the finest and flashiest reviewers, so I make an escape and can just start another instrument, praying that I have truly heard something.

When introduced to the Lacanian likes of you, Anouchka, I felt, even more than felt, that your toolbox contained things that are acute, precise, and gentle.

'The purest form of listening is to listen without memory or desire.'
– Wilfred Bion

Can there be such thing as an art of listening? What kind of art, or craft, could it be? There's no obvious product, no tangible object to demonstrate that listening has taken place. Still, we might agree that one can distinguish between a good and bad listener, or at least good and bad listening.

What is it possible to say about this impalpable but vital activity? Is it an activity at all, or maybe more of a passivity? Does its apparent passivity make it any less of a *thing*? Rather than falling for the simple binaries of active/passive, speaker/hearer, or even perpetrator/victim (which might sound extreme, but I'm sure you've been on the receiving end of a deadly boring monologue), perhaps it's possible instead to think of listening as a provocation or instigation. Why would anyone attempt to make a meaningful sound if they didn't have the idea that there was a pre-existing, complementary space in which it might be worth their while to lodge it? What if it were listeners who incited speakers to speak – or musicians to play, writers to write, composers to compose – rather than vice versa?

•

Let's start with Patient A, Anna O., real name Bertha Pappenheim, the world's first analysand. She is famously credited with coining the phrase 'the talking cure'. We might ask what gave her the idea that talking helped.

Was it really the talking, or the listening? And how did the two intertwine?

According to Freud's biographer, Ernest Jones, Pappenheim was 'an unusually intelligent girl of twenty-one, who developed a museum of symptoms in connexion with her father's fatal illness. Among them were paralysis of three limbs with contractures and anaesthesias, severe and complicated disturbances of sight and speech, inability to take food and a distressing, nervous cough'. More than that, she would slip into weird, excitable states and then, thanks to the practice of self-hypnosis, snap back to her normal self again. The family called in Dr Josef Breuer to see if there was anything he could do. Breuer began a series of twilight visits, coinciding with Pappenheim's daily moments of greatest sanity. One day she described to him the onset of one of her symptoms and subsequently found that it had completely vanished. Breuer was amazed, and perhaps it was this gratifying response of his that caused his fascinating patient to repeat the process again and again.

Things carried on this way for over a year until Breuer's wife became jealous, ground down by innumerable stories of Pappenheim's miraculous – albeit seemingly endless – recovery. This 'provoked a violent reaction in [Breuer], perhaps compounded of love and guilt', and he proceeded as if he himself were being snapped out of a trance. He abruptly terminated the sessions – causing his patient to experience a violent relapse – before vanishing on holiday with his wife and immediately getting her pregnant.

The whole experience frightened Breuer away from psychoanalytic work; that kind of listening was just too risky. Pappenheim, however, was prepared to give it one more go, with Freud himself, some years later. This time it went well and she concluded – perhaps thanks to Freud's greater sensitivity to what he came to call 'transference' – that some psychoanalysts are better at it than others.

While Breuer's naivety about the explosive potential of listening led to an abrupt, catastrophic end to the treatment, he and Pappenheim nonetheless opened the way to Freudian analysis, the plethora of modern talking cures, and, most recently, therapy bots.

There are a number of commonsensical ideas about what constitutes listening well – patience, tolerance, availability, responsiveness, lack of moral judgement. But weren't these precisely what Dr Breuer offered? And didn't it end in tears?

•

In the mid 1960s, Joseph Weizenbaum developed the first chatbot, christened ELIZA after the parroting pro-tagonist of George Bernard Shaw's *Pygmalion*. ELIZA was designed to respond like a Rogerian, human-centred therapist, mainly repeating people's words back to them, slightly differently inflected. Weizenbaum hadn't set out with any desire to replace flawed, sentimental human therapists with robots. He'd simply designed the soft-ware to provide a framework enabling research into human/machine verbal interactions. The linguistic con-ventions of Rogerian therapy were conveniently boring enough to be programmed into a 1960s computer. On the bright side, there seemed very little risk that ELIZA would fall in love with anyone, nor they with her. (Fans of the 2013 film *Her* might disagree.) In that sense she was safe, if a little limited. Surprisingly, however, people seemed to really like talking – or typing – to her, using her implacable digital stupidity to enable them to say things they'd never dare say to another sentient being.

Weizenbaum was horrified that his creation was so well-received and went on to become a forceful critic of AI, stating that the idea that 'a computer can be pro-grammed to become an effective psychotherapist' was 'perverse' and that it was pure hubris to believe that ma-chines could be designed to simulate the full range of human intelligence. More than that, the corresponding belief that humans are basically sophisticated robots – we just haven't yet cracked our full computational code – seemed to jeopardise the complexity of our lived experience. If we began to equate people with computers we'd be pushed towards situations where computers might be used to control us, underpinned by the premise that if they are like us, we should also be like them. If they can contain their non-existent feelings, for example, why can't we?

If this sounded a little fanciful, even hysterical, in the 1960s, some of Weizenbaum's predictions are already borne out by the use of digital therapists by the UK National Health Service and the fact that many of us voluntarily have mindfulness apps installed on our phones, unwaveringly reminding us not to get swept up in 'unnecessary' emotions.

If Josef Breuer's listening was somehow too much – his patient fell madly in love with him, causing him to run away in panic – and ELIZA's listening risked being too little – the software just offered a vapid semblance of a human response – what would be just right?

•

'Do you picture the psychoanalyst as a man leaning forward in his chair, watching with all five senses for minute psychological signs, anxious lest one should escape him? I've talked about tiny signals, the faint stimuli that flit and waver. [...] In the face of such differentiated data, so hard to take hold of, you would think that the keenest attention is called for. Do you imagine the analyst not just attentive but tense? The picture is false. '
– Theodor Reik, *Listening with The Third Ear*

The question of how to listen became gradually more pressing for Freud and his circle as they created the job of professional listener. Of course doctors, priests, and faith healers had been doing it for years, but they would tend to follow up their listening with a definite course of action – surgery, Hail Marys, rituals. Psycho-analysis was different in that the quality of the listening was foregrounded. The listening itself explicitly formed part of the cure. The trick was somehow to listen in a way that enabled the other person to hear themselves afresh. In order to do this, Freud developed the idea that the analyst's 'evenly suspended attention' should form a counterpart to the analysand's free association. In much the same way that patients were instructed to speak without editing, analytic technique 'consist[ed] simply in not directing one's notice to anything in particular'. This way the analyst would not only avoid exhausting themselves, but would have a greater hope of not letting their prejudices about what's worthwhile or interesting get in the way of what they were able to hear. Sometimes they might not realise what was important until later. Or ever.

Sándor Ferenczi's 1928 paper 'The Elasticity of Psycho-Analytic Technique' broaches the possibility of psycho-analysis as a standardisable craft. If people were often tempted to see Freud and his followers as freakishly brilliant observers of the hidden corners of the human psyche, Ferenczi is here to tell us that it is 'an undeniable advance that analysis has gradually succeeded in putting tools for the more delicate investigation of the kind into the hands of the physician and student of only average gifts'. This dubious improvement is partly put down to the publication of Freud's 'Papers on Technique' (1911–15) – a list of mainly negative recommendations, or things not to do – and also to the 'second fundamental rule of psycho-analysis' (the first being that the patient must speak freely) that 'anyone who wishes to undertake anal-ysis must first be analysed himself'. In theory, this would make a person more able to listen without internal inter-ference. Of course Ferenczi was writing a decade before the publication of Freud's rather gloomy pronouncement on psychoanalytic practice 'Psychoanalysis Terminable and Interminable', after which it became less plausible to claim that analysed people were saner and 'more in control of the inevitable weaknesses and peculiarities of [their] own character[s]' than others.

One of the thornier issues brought out by Ferenczi is when to interpret and when to shut up. If you go in too strong you may upset the patient, or even lose them altogether, but if you remain silent you also risk the same. His answer to this conundrum is the somewhat imprecise notion of 'psychological tact', which he equates with empathy. The practitioner apparently needs to have a good radar for what the patient can take. You have to develop a feeling for when to be confrontational and when to sit back. But in case this sounds like he's putting psychoanalytic listening back in the hands of people who just happen to be good at it, he's also an advocate of humility, stating, 'the analyst's modesty must be no studied pose, but a reflection of the limitations of our knowledge'. Even if we were great at the work we couldn't, or shouldn't, know it.

In short, nothing in the theory can guarantee good listening. It appears to remain a talent, or accident, that retains an element of mystery. In other words, perhaps, more of an art than a craft.

•

In 1953, Jacques Lacan presented his 'Rome Discourse', a treatise on psychoanalytic training that broke with many of the traditions of the post-Freudians while simultaneously recommending a 'return to Freud'. In it, he argues for an attention to the machinations of language and the ways in which these play out in the subject's discourse. He recommends that trainee analysts do cryptic crosswords in order to attune themselves to the various confounding ways in which meaning may be transmitted, distorted, or interrupted. Instead of the blurry notions of tact, empathy, and baffling 'third ears' (a concept he pokes fun at in passing), Lacan suggests a more rigorous, linguistic approach to the ways in which the rules and materiality of language – not to mention the fact that it is imposed on each of us from the outside – have a profound impact on what we then go on to do with it.

In case this sounds like he is advocating a cold, logical outlook, Lacan portrays language and speech as infused with trauma, loss, enjoyment, perversity – anything but a computer-like input/output of information. Language may be a technology, but in the hands, mouths, and ears of humans it can't help but be fleshed out, bled into, contaminated, stained, and debauched. So, in Lacanian analysis, when we listen out for homonyms, puns, inadvertent neologisms – and point these out to the analysand – we are simultaneously attuned to the libidinised aspects of language, the fact that it is liable to be infused with enjoyment, perplexity, and disgust.

In order to understand why this might be the case, it's helpful to look at Lacan's notion of the 'invocatory drive' – the drive to listen and be listened to. While for Freud there were three drives – the oral, the anal, and the genital – Lacan adds in two more: the scopic and the invocatory, concerned with the eyes and the ears. While Freud's drives link with the organs and forces that cause us to eat, excrete, and breed, Lacan points out the importance of looking and listening in our formation as human beings. Seeing and being seen, speaking and listening are all of vital importance to social existence. They are how we learn to understand (and, perhaps more importantly, misunderstand) ourselves in the context of other visible, verbal entities. Of course, one can be unable to see or to hear and still get on in the world, but the missing sense(s) will need to be supplemented by the available ones. People born without the capacity either to see or to hear may need to rely heavily on touch – and their own ingenuity and that of their caregivers – to become communicative beings. This might suggest that a haptic drive needs to be added to the other five.

For both Freud and Lacan, while these drives may link to biological needs, they can't be equated with 'instincts'.

An instinct may cause a creature to behave in a life-sustaining way – to follow movement, to crawl towards water, to eat dung – without ever having seen another creature do the same, but a human drive is more convoluted. Our sexual drives may tend towards non-procreative aims, we may prefer to starve ourselves than to eat, or to eat food that is almost entirely non-nutritious. The link between the drive and its object is anything but natural or inevitable. To intensify the matter, we live in cultures that further sway our preferences in a variety of directions, perhaps none more so than late-capitalist societies that seem to offer ever-less nourishing options for consumption. Since the invention of the internet, our drives might land us pretty much anywhere.

A fundamental drive to hear and be heard would then be as mutable, unpredictable, and beholden to the caprices of our early experiences as any of the other four. Our relationship with our own voices and words, and the voices and words of others, could be anything. The very particular modes in which our early caregivers responded and failed to respond to us forms the kinds of speakers and listeners we become. Perhaps we prefer to sing or scream than to articulate carefully. We love opera and hate political debate. We feel at our least alienated when listening to a certain style of jazz. We think in lists, or tend to alliterate. We can't bear to leave pauses. We think cellos are better than violins. We can't love anyone with an English accent. Our capacity to engage with sound and meaning is shot through with the contingencies of the ways in which the world has acted on us, and our attempts at coming to terms with whatever that was. In short, as Breuer was slow to recognise, speaking and listening can't help getting bound up with attachment and satisfaction (aka love and sex).

All this complicates the idea of generic good or bad listening. One person's charmingly undivided attention will be another person's invasively scrutinising hell. The idea of a standardisation of the craft of listening, à la Ferenczi, seems ever less probable. In 1936, having scanned the literature to try to deduce whether some talking therapies work better than others, the psychologist Saul Rosenzweig introduced the term 'Dodo Bird', after the bird in Lewis Carroll's *Alice in Wonderland* who announces at the end of a race, 'Everyone has won, and all must have prizes'. The Dodo Bird Verdict has since become a loosely accepted notion in the therapy world. Of course, there are qualifiers – some therapies are thought to work better with some conditions than others, but even the qualifiers require more qualifiers, so much so that the simplicity of the Dodo Bird Verdict still generally ends up being the most satisfactory overall idea. Still, more recent research into the efficacy of the various forms of talking therapy seems to produce a striking result. While all the different modalities, from short-term, directive Cognitive Behavioural Therapy to long-term, speculative psychoanalysis seem to fare equally well in terms of (to put it horribly) client satisfaction, it seems that some individual practitioners are more highly thought of than others, irrespective of their theoretical angle. More important than your knowledge of this or that theory, apparently, is your capacity to form strong working alliances with your patients (as B.A. Arnow et al and F. Falkenström et al argue), and to be good at noticing when these might be at risk of going awry and may need a little extra attention (as J.D. Safran and J.C. Muran suggest). In short, you need to be very alive to the effects of the therapy on the people you work with, and to be quick, clever, and intuitive in your responses to these effects.

•

'Listen to others, even the dull and the ignorant. They too have their story.'
– Desiderata

A Couch in New York (1996), Chantal Akerman's brilliant cinematic flop, tells the story of a 'good' and a 'bad' psychoanalyst. Henry, played by William Hurt, lives in a fancy New York apartment, paid for by his career as an urbane, book-writing shrink. In spite of his success, he's bored with his life as the paid ear to a series of entitled, suit-wearing men. Desperate for temporary respite from his unlikeable patients, he responds to an advertisement for a house-swap in Paris. He lands in the bohemian dive of Béatrice (Juliette Binoche) and, more importantly, she is transported to Manhattan, where Henry's patients – all of whom seem to have suppressed the idea that an analyst can take a holiday – keep turning up for sessions. The patients go on talking to Béatrice, deciding she must be Henry's holiday cover. As it turns out, she has a propensity for dealing with grumpy men (indeed Henry has to deal with parallel incursions from her stroppy boyfriends) and takes a great interest in the details of their misery, often chipping in with examples and observations from her own life.

Happily, Béatrice has a friend in New York who gives her a crash course in how to be a proper psychoanalyst: repeat everything they say back in a deadpan voice and never give in to the transference. Béatrice somehow puts this together with her irrepressible inclination to have a really good chat. She lurches, seemingly uncontrollably, between a parody of semi-robotic standard practice and outlandishly heartfelt responsiveness. The patients love it. They all agree she's much better at it than Henry. Even Henry, who disguises himself as a patient in order to work out what she's up to, finds himself able to access lost memories and feelings in her presence. Needless to say, they fall in love (which is, of course, strictly not allowed according to the rules of the helpful friend).

While it might be unwise to use a fictional example to prove a point, the film argues for a kind of inspired listening that may embolden therapists who want to avoid the caricature of the well-trained, well-regulated therapeutic automaton. Bion's famous recommendation to listen 'without memory or desire' is all very well, but isn't that exactly what machines are so good at? The film's suggestion that it's a person's defects and idiosyncrasies that make them capable of effective or affecting listening makes perfect, poetic sense.

•

We can find a real-world example of the kind of listening that might actually make a difference in Claudia Rankine's *Just Us: An American Conversation* (2020). In this collection of essays and poems, the author gives accounts of conversations and experiences she's had with White friends and strangers where the subject of race has disrupted the course of a previously harmonious interaction. In the middle of an otherwise enjoyable chat, a man on an aeroplane suddenly announces, 'I don't see colour', in spite of the fact that he's just told her he has been working on diversity in his job. Rankine recounts: 'The phrase "I don't see colour" pulled an emergency brake in my brain'. The fact that she can see – and feel – the problem, while he apparently can't, immediately threatens to drive a wedge between them. Still, they're stuck together on a flight so there's little opportunity to walk away. In a moment of startling quick-wittedness, Rankine responds by paraphrasing of Sojourner Truth: 'Ain't I a black woman?' she asks. He is quick to grasp what she's saying and asks what other idiotic things he's said so far. From here they begin a correspondence that includes her showing him the article she wrote about their interaction, and his response to the article, which in turn causes her to think further about her own acceptance of his privileged account of race.

In another example, Rankine and a White friend go to see *Fairview* by Jackie Sibblies Drury – a play which culminates in a Black actor requesting that the White members of the audience get up onto the stage. The friend doesn't move, and Rankine describes feeling betrayed. For weeks they don't speak. Again, Rankine writes about the experience and shows the piece to her friend, after which she receives a pained email in which the friend affirms Rankine's description of what happened, before going on to describe her own confusion about White people's moral masochism and the idea that we can somehow pay off our guilt by owning it publicly. Rankine generously accepts the friend's position. The story is as much about Rankine's own shift from incomprehension to cautious acceptance as it is about the friend's perplexing inertia. And, like the first story, it clearly shows how people may be positioned to hear things completely differently and can gain a great deal from having their own listening both supplemented and destabilised by the listening of another.

Rather like Ferenczi, Rankine asks herself whether to remain silent or whether to challenge. Here we see two instances where the challenge went well. Like a good analyst, she enables people to hear themselves differently. But more than that, she allows their responses to open up further questions for herself. Rather than remaining stuck in one position, or simply correcting other people's errors, she suggests it may be perfectly possible for people to affect each other, to hear and alter each other, without it being a catastrophe.

One of the problems with listening is that it's impossible to start with a clean slate. If you're listening to words being spoken in the context of a culture – yours, someone else's, or neither – then your understanding is warped before you even begin. The question is simply when or how will it show?

In the aftermath of George Floyd's murder and the eruption of Black Lives Matter protests across the world, Cressida Dick, then the British Chief of Police, found herself on the national news trying to defend the British police force's record on racism. She suggested that it was only the Americans who had a problem and that good old British bobbies are generally great, apart from a couple of dodgy ones who will be sure to have their comeuppance because nobody likes a racist. She couldn't entertain the idea that the British police might be structurally, institutionally racist. The interviewer kept pressing her over and over again, and she kept going with the party line, keeping a totally straight face except for one moment, when she was asked about the possibility of unconscious racism. Here she batted the idea off as completely ridiculous, tittering that there was no need for the police force to have Unconscious Bias Training.

It's quite unusual to see Cressida Dick laugh, so it aroused my curiosity, especially as one component of the idea she was laughing at – the unconscious – is a core concept of psychoanalysis. Of course, I wouldn't be so presumptuous as to guess whether it was racism, or bias, or Freudian theory that she found funny, but her laugh stuck out as a strange thing.

One possibility is that she's so on top of the discourse that she was simply laughing at the idea that Unconscious Bias Training does any good at all. That is an idea that seems easier to get behind. When public figures rush off to get their unconscious racism sorted out we probably all know what it's like to smirk a little. Some of the problems with Unconscious Bias Training, at least as it's administered at the moment, are not unlike the problems with listening raised by Ferenczi. It depends on the idea that a person can become mentally 'clean' enough to listen in a pure and unbiased way. And, once they have heard something that makes their ears prick up, that they can learn to present it back to the other person in such a way that they can bear to hear it too.

The current mainstream solution to structural racism is liable to sound a little funny to anyone with any experience of working in clinical psychotherapy or analysis, or who has been in analysis themselves and knows how hard it is to change the ways people think and act. Sending people on short, corporate courses where they confess to their inevitable, unavoidable racism might not be the best way to get the job done. Not to say it's all bad, just that it might not be the panacea that it briefly seemed to be treated as. You certainly hear enough about it from people of all racial and ethnic backgrounds, not just bolshy White people, who find it infuriating, patronising, inappropriate, and pathetic for any number of different reasons, and not necessarily simply because of their resistance.

Tackling racism is plainly an urgent project and getting individuals to take responsibility for their own racism is a straightforward and sensible thing to try. But how you go about it is another matter. Callout culture, hectoring people, and trying to infuse them with shame might not be the best options. Psychoanalysts are well placed to say this because if we tried that stuff with our analysands we'd be left with a handful of hardcore masochists after everybody else had left.

This isn't obvious to all psychoanalysts. If you look back into the history of psychoanalysis, hectoring and shaming people has had a prominent place in huge swathes of analytic practice. Indeed, this is often what people think a psychoanalyst is: someone who calls you out on your dodgy drives and wishes. This is why strangers sometimes run away from analysts at parties; they think you'll be some smart alec who can see immediately, and will tell them, that they want to fuck their mum or kill their sister. In this sense, having an Oedipus complex is something like having unconscious racist attitudes – it's structural. Pointing it out to people as if you've discovered their big secret is liable either to piss them off and make them defensive, or cow them into a position of guilt and shame. None of which is helpful to people who are the object of racism, nor to people suffering from guilt about their sexuality.

Here it is helpful to look at a paper by Mike Noon that brings together a lot of research on the failure of UBT, 'Pointless Diversity Training: Unconscious Bias, New Racism and Agency' (2017). Noon begins with an account of the current state of racism in the UK. Since the 1980s, blatant racism has been largely reprimanded, so people have been forced to find more covert ways to express it. Noon organises racism into two general categories. The first is the cluster he calls 'New Racism', which includes 'symbolic racism', 'modern racism', and 'colour-blind racism' (this last is an idea brilliantly drawn up in a 2002 paper by Eduardo Bonilla-Silva called 'The Linguistics of Color Blind Racism: How to Talk Nasty about Blacks without Sounding "Racist"'). New Racism is a slippery category because the people whose behaviour would fall under it are quite self-aware about their racism, although they don't exactly take responsibility for it. They think that racism is inevitable and acquired through misinformation in childhood, bad comedy, bad friends, stereotyping. They know that you don't become racist through actual bad experiences with actual Black and Brown people, it just seeps into you from everywhere. Still, there's a belief that racism proper is no longer really a thing, that it's been dealt with because, look, no one says anything racist anymore. In fact, minorities should stop kicking up such a fuss because it alienates people and is counterproductive.

The harm of this sort of racism is perpetrated stealthily by people not complying with things like diversity initiatives at work, or by being silent on the subject, or denying that it *is* a subject. People in this category tend to be unaffected by Unconscious Bias Training as they are so *au fait* with the topic of unconscious bias: 'We know everyone's a bit racist but we're all doing our best and soon it will be completely sorted'. They don't mind admitting to the vestiges of their racism, therefore training doesn't make them go off and think about their attitudes. The whole thing comes as no surprise, so it's just an annoying way to spend an afternoon. In fact, for people in this camp, it's a total waste of money; Robin DiAngelo charges many thousands of dollars for her workshops, and modern racists will use this fact to further discredit their usefulness.

On the other hand there is 'Aversive Racism'. Aversive racists are outspokenly anti-racist and egalitarian. As Noon puts it, 'deep down they hold negative beliefs about racial minorities due to discomfort or anxiety stemming from their own sociocultural influences. As a consequence their actions and behaviour manifest a subtle racism.' This might show itself when discrimination against a certain group can be justified on non-racialised grounds, for instance for business reasons: 'We can't let in refugees because there are already enough disenfranchised people here who need our help', for example. Or when there's an opportunity to give members of their own group preferential treatment over other people.

Because these people ostensibly don't know that they are racist there might be some mileage in giving them Unconscious Bias Training. However, on mainstream UBT trainings the drift is to point out that racism is immoral and illegal and can therefore land your business with a financial penalty. If people firmly believe that they are non-racist then none of these problems need pointing out to them. They might say things like, 'My niece is mixed race so I can't possibly be racist'. Unlike with the New Racists, there might at least be a surprise factor in discovering that they do in fact hold unconscious racist ideas, which they might discover by using the Harvard Test, for example, which asserts that 85% of White people are biased against Black people. Still, the person might not accept the results of the test or, just as bad, might be so ashamed of the exposure of their racism that they begin to pull away from any encounters with people from other groups. They become so frightened of making a racist Freudian slip that they steer clear of any situation that puts them at risk of being accidentally outed.

In either of these cases, the problem with UBT is that it makes a muddle of conscious and unconscious, assuming people have full agency and will take responsibility for their unconscious if you tell them that this is what they have to do. On the other hand, by setting racism up as an unconscious issue, it encourages them to disavow responsibility. Racism, they might argue, is just in the ether and we are infected with it before we can even think or speak for ourselves. Therefore every little bit we do against it is already more than enough.

For Noon, UBT falls short because it fails to understand agency, responsibility, and how these might relate to unconsciously held ideas. Like early Freudians, UBT trainers think you just have to tell people what's in their unconscious – to name it – and then everything will get better. The person's decency will step in and take over where the unconscious left off.

The American psychoanalyst Bernard Apfelbaum argues for a very simple but also challenging and surprisingly mind-bending way of thinking about how to change people's minds. In a paper called 'Analysing, Not Psycho-analysing', he writes about how to interpret without being a jerk. In this sense it's a very important paper. Apfelbaum utterly lambasts pretty much all psychoanalytic modalities, not for their underlying theories – he's fully Freudian – but for their counterproductive modes of intervening. His ideas might suggest ways of tackling unconscious bias without resorting to callout culture or Robin DiAngelo-esque patronising bossiness, and of listening and responding in ways that open things up rather than shut them down.

Apfelbaum describes how to help analysands suffer less – how to avoid the 'negative therapeutic reaction' (i.e., thinking therapy, or your individual therapist, is terrible) that not only crops up in numerous analyses, but could also be said to have been triggered by psychoanalysis out in the world. People hate psychoanalysis because they think it involves some smug person in a comfortable armchair telling you why you're wrong to think or feel the way you do. But all over the literature you see the negative therapeutic reaction being held up as proof of the *rightness* of an interpretation. If an analysand is angry or offended, you've got them. That's the work: good for you, you're a brilliant analyst. If they can't take it, they're a terrible patient. In fact, instead of thinking about how one might be able to work differently in different cases, the point in analysis became only to work with people whose egos were stable enough to take a good kicking.

The negative therapeutic reaction is the basis of what Apfelbaum terms 'id analysis', which entails naming what the id (loosely speaking, the untamed drives) is up to so that the patient can see beyond the surface of their complaint to the conflicts and drives that are being siphoned through it. You hate your boss because you secretly love them, or because you identify with them, or they're just like your dad, or all three. Of course, some patients – psychotic or so-called 'borderline' people – won't be able to take this, so you can just treat them with kindness and care. Therapy, which is supposedly less heroic than analysis, is simply about containment. So you're horrible to the neurotics, nice to the psychotics. Psychoanalytic patients are seen as a bunch of pesky people who are trying to get stuff past you, and it's your job to stop them being so pesky. (This is also pretty much the tone of Robin DiAngelo's book *White Fragility*.)

Apfelbaum asks what might happen if you turn this idea around. Instead of trying to name what's going on with the id, you try to name what's going on in the ego. Rather than naming the disturbing, repressed thing, you name the painful tangles that people get themselves into while trying to moderate everything and appear reasonable. He gives an example from a paper by Hanna Segal, in which a new trainee analyst is saying he wants to study and get on with the work as soon as he can, then goes on to speak about some digestive troubles he's having, and also mentions cows. Hanna Segal says, in her first session with him: 'I am the cow, like the mother who breast fed you: you feel that you are going to empty me greedily, as fast as possible, of all my analysismilk'. It's a classic example of going straight in with a 'deep' interpretation. The patient immediately starts to confess to guilt about exhausting and exploiting his mother, and Hanna Segal feels like she's done some gold-standard analytic work.

Apfelbaum mentions other examples where patients are upset by interpretations, although that doesn't seem to have been the case, insofar as we know, in this instance. In this particular case, the analysand at least knows what he's in for if he's enrolled on a Kleinian training. As Apfelbaum says: '[he] undoubtedly knew that Kleinians says these things to people all day long; you shouldn't take it too personally.'

In an instance like this, Apfelbaum's idea would be to focus instead on the person's awkwardness about presenting himself to his analyst as a psychoanalytic candidate.

Maybe he feels guilty about the idea that he is saying he thinks he could do her job just as well as she can. Perhaps he feels ashamed of his embarrassment about the sexual fantasies he's going to have to reveal to her; if he's saying he wants to be a psychoanalyst, perhaps he thinks he needs to be less of a pussy about his own sexuality. Perhaps he's worried that he'll be a boring patient. For Apfelbaum, this is the stuff you need to work with. You have to let the analysand have their problems, to acknowledge all the guilt and shame experienced in the ego. In other words, you're better off working towards helping a person out with the viciousness of their superego. This is what would actually be illuminating and alleviating. If you just clap them round the head with their unacceptable drives and unconscious phantasies you'll be in league with their superego against them, and what use is that?

Apfelbaum is talking about a much kinder way of listening and responding: a method he also argues is far more effective, not to mention more interesting. It doesn't have the brutal common sense of 'tell them what's wrong with them so they can sort themselves out' but is more nuanced. Apfelbaum says:

> The implicit or explicit assumption [of id analysis] is that what makes people change is to realise that they are being bad. In other words, we assume that the way to change people is to be disapproving. Why do we assume that? Because that's how our parents treated us and how everyone else has always treated us.

His idea is to develop a new mode of intervening along completely different lines. However, 'It's only when you try not to be an id analyst that you discover how difficult it is not to be.' It's easy enough to set yourself up as a heroic opponent to people's faulty ideas and assumptions. This is what you see in many 'corrective' forms of therapy, but also in Unconscious Bias Trainings and books like *White Fragility*. The problem is that these forms of super-egoic lashing invariably either stir up commensurate defences or leave people feeling helpless. What seems much harder to do is to place yourself in such a way as to accompany people out of the thought processes that make their own and other people's lives a misery. As opposed to the assertive, even combative, therapists who proudly refuse to collude with their clients, Apfelbaum is proposing that we see ourselves as companions rather than opponents.

In Sherry Turkle's book *Alone Together*, we are invited to consider a near future in which human interactions are seen as so troubling and unsatisfying that they are slowly but surely being supplanted by infinitely preferable exchanges with machines. She describes meeting teenagers who prefer the sense of control provided by texting to the unnerving free flow of live conversation. She speaks to a woman in an old people's home whose loneliness and depression is supposedly being ameliorated by the company of a fluffy, animatronic pet. She comes across men and women who say they would prefer to date a love robot than a live human (flesh-and-blood partners being too untrustworthy). She is taken to task by a journalist for her intolerant attitude towards human/machine romantic relations – he compares her to a homophobe because she can't easily accept the idea of people marrying robots.

Turkle asks what will happen if we accede too willingly to the idea that interactions with machines are a viable replacement for human-to-human contact. While we might rid ourselves of the downside of engaging with people who lie to us or let us down, we also risk losing the excitement that comes with spontaneously liking or being liked, being interested and inspiring interest, or otherwise being taken by surprise by the interplay of thoughts and feelings we trigger in others and they in us.

Towards the end of the book, Turkle writes about an academic friend who has been in a serious car accident and needs complex care. He has an interest in robots and sees how they might be able to help people in his situation. He then goes on to describe some of his human carers, who are a mixture of inept and actively cruel. He describes being pulled along by his hair in one instance, by his tubes in another. 'A robot would never do that,' he says. 'But, you know, in the end, that person who dragged me by my tubes had a story. I could find out about it.' He seems to argue that dignity is somehow tied to authenticity. Turkle concludes: 'Although he would not want his life endangered, he prefers the sadist to the robot.'

•

This takes us back to the chicken-and-eggness of the relationship between speaking and listening. Who does what to whom?

As Walter J. Ong tells us in *Orality and Literacy*, his sublime meditation on the relations of sounds to sense, and sense to life, death, humanity, and inhumanity:

> In real human communication, the sender has to be not only in the sender position but also in the receiver position before he or she can send anything. [...] I have to sense something in the other's mind to which my own utterance can relate. Human communication is never one-way. Always, it not only calls for response but is shaped in its very form and content by anticipated response.

Speaking and listening are inextricable. Both are forms of mind-reading – shot through with all the unreliability that this would suggest. What you say is dictated by what you think the other person will be able to hear. What you hear will be governed by what you think the other person is trying to tell you. Both your speaking and your listening will be inflected by everything you've heard and said before. And somehow in this cacophony of guesswork, trial, and error, something that we loosely call 'meaning' may migrate between one body and another. Speech, and listening, are forms of touch. Bertha Pappenheim was surely touched by Breuer's attentiveness. Turkle's texting teenagers perhaps fear the intrusion and intimacy of communication untamed. But how lonely might they find themselves if they actually succeeded in muting other minds?

We might conclude that it's the flesh, the failings and flaws of the listener that ultimately make them adequate to the task. While therapy bots might be ever-ready, tireless and implacable, if we are to feel properly heard, perhaps it needs to be by another being subject to the same drives, limits, uncertainties, excitements and failings as us. The one thing worse than bad listening is perfect listening. Although we may be erratic beasts, we are probably still less frightening than the impeccable immortals that threaten to displace us. The gentle warmth of an ear, with its ridges, pads and sticky cavities has never seemed more precious.

Derrida's Wire Tap, Coppola's Conversation
Precursors to Pegasus

Surveillance is for now a naked, feathered horse
grounded for one news cycle onto the front page of
every techno-illuminated broadsheet.

The pixelated Pegasus, equestrian eavesdropper is
here lifted out of the electronic ether and into
its proper place; center stage in the dramaturgy
of listening.

For half a reel of hailstorms we can hear a patched
history of this furtive gelding, until it takes flight
in a new form and we can quietly attend to those at
work and whispering out of earshot in the wings.

Can I hear you, if we are unheard by horses?

'My 'at home' is also constituted by the field of access via my telephone line (through which I can give my time, my word, my friendship, my love, my help, to whomever I wish, and so invite whomever I wish to come into my home, first in my ear, when I wish, at any time of day or night, whether the other is my across-the-fence neighbor, a fellow citizen, or any other friend or person I don't know at the other end of the world). Now if my "home," in principle inviolable, is also constituted, and in a more essential, interior way, by my phone line, but also my e-mail, but also my fax, but also my access to the Internet, then the intervention of the [listening] State becomes a violation of the inviolable, in the place where inviolable immunity remains the condition of hospitality.'
– Jacques Derrida

On 10 January 1996, when Derrida was delivering this idea in a seminar, one still needed a physical space with a wire coming into it to go online. Those with access at the time (4% of those in the global north) spent an average of thirty minutes per month surfing what was universally called the World Wide Web. One sensed its arachnid aspect and was riding a thread in the times one was connected. Most phones still hung on the wall and were tied to the place they were used by a copper filament that entered through a hole. The wire here was a kind of window through which voices passed, eyes gazed, and listening happened.

> But current technological developments are restructuring space in such a way that what constitutes a space of controlled and circumscribed property

is just what opens it to intrusion. That, once again, is not absolutely new: in order to constitute the space of a habitable house and a home, you also need an opening, a door and windows, you have to give up a passage to the outside world [*l'étranger*]. There is no house or interior without a door or windows.

In anticipation of Pegasus spyware, the year Derrida was recorded uttering the above was also the year in which the term Cloud Computing first appeared. The twine through the wall making a physical window and allowing us to speak on the tin can phone of the early internet was about to be cut. The world wide web soon went the way of the human voice when it first hit the airwaves and was brought into the home on the radio – wireless. No longer a line.

The sinister sense of wireless, cloud-based surveillance, with its slashed webs, broken threads, and all walls turned into windows (possibly of one-way glass), leave what, for us, in the way of listening? Is listening the act of tying or retying a thread, connecting ourselves to a web, pulling tight the twine between two people so we can whisper into the tin cans we hold to our ears to make out at least a few words?

The Sanskrit word for 'what is heard' is *Shruti*. It is a central term in textual analysis and has a kaleidoscope of related and applied meanings. It turns upon music and the quarter-tone, the oral tradition and the thread between sacred utterances; it means an offering, the gift of one's ear, drawing a line with an implement, cutting the earth and illuminating a path, and it also means the falling of snow.

One of the most notable things about snow is the resounding silence.

So how to start hearing you in *Shruti*'s snowfield?

In 1974, when high end recording meant owning, or at least
having access to reel-to-reel tape, the inventor of the term "sound
design," Walter Murch, was put to work on a film about listening.
Francis Ford Coppola wanted to fuse the concept of Antonioni's "Blow Up"
with the world of audio surveillance. Its central charachter, Henry
Caul (born in one? like the Dalai Lama and mythical for sailors,
meaning he cannot drown - in voices?) is awash from the outset in sound
 that he masterfully filters on half inch tape. Reel-to-reel is a
moniker added to his chosen form of technology in the 1950's to distinguish this form of recording from other applications of magnetic ribbon.
These included the endless loop cassette (let the band play on) data
sinks for signals from Hydrogen Bombs and drives for information
storage on early mainframe computers. Until then it needed no special
name as the only tape in town, with human generated sounds as its
mandate to capture. One of the main features of magnetic tape is that
the speed at which it runs, the faster the better, determines the
quality of the recording, along with enhanced width. A thumb wide
stripe ripping over a tape head assembly at high speed will offer a
better account of conversational happenings than something spare,
focused and slow. This is so unlike sitting before a human speaker
and using our ears and attention to slowly narrow the flatline of our
awareness to their voice, and more in their voice - not pulling a
runner carpet's width of added capture and over determination into our
attempt at hearing.

   Henry Caul is a clandestine, mercenary wire tapper who is caught
by one delicately recorded Conversation and brought through sound,
mind and murder into reel/real listening. His respite, until then,
from hired honing into the word choices and inflections of others is
playing the saxophone. Perhaps here we hear his voice, begging through
a brass pipe, and not when he is dryly describing the details of his
job and the equipment he uses to spy on other's emotions in their
lucratively human soundscape of exchanges.

I'm not sure how cut out I am to be a vampire. Vampires don't seem particularly interested in reciprocity and consent. I've invited Robert to take part in writing this book and I want him to be comfortable. It's odd that I asked him to say something about Derrida on hospitality and now I fear being inhospitable to him in this space. The last thing I want to do is to stress him out or embarrass him. I want him to write his own thing in his own way, to let him be Robert, but is it OK that I go on so much and he's so laconic? Or that we have such different styles? I'm journalistic while he's poetic. Is it acceptable that I take so much space and he takes so little? Then again it's not like I can squeeze words out of him, even though his leg is now better and we are free to meet.

I'm not at all sure what I imagined collaborating on writing would be like. I'd always puzzled over Deleuze and Guattari, Laplanche and Pontalis, Matt Stone and Trey Parker. How do they do it? By what process? Does one tend to dominate? What if they disagree? While I'm still sure Robert can teach me something about listening, I'm not sure how to bring it about, nor how to demonstrate it here.

Last week I attended a meeting of Indigenous elders who had been invited to COP26 and then neither listened to nor allowed into any important meetings. A concerned theatre director had invited them to London and provided them with an audience and a microphone. They argued forcefully that their voices needed to be heard as they were good at living on planet Earth without destroying it. Over and over again they stressed the importance of listening. In the audience, we listened and felt absolutely helpless. It was devastating. Afterwards, audience and speakers went to the bar and had a really good party, with interpreters. Everyone felt deeply affected by what they'd heard but found it hard to know what to do. Still, it was probably marginally better that the elders went home having finally been heard.

Listening certainly seems to involve responsibility on both sides. Sometimes it can even be a real burden. Presumably that's why the politicians and fossil fuel lobbyists at COP kept the Indigenous people on the wrong side of the door; having heard what they have to say you become the carrier of it. If you want to stay rich it's better not to hear it. Listening is risky.

On a much smaller scale, am I able to let Robert have his own voice here? What am I hoping to get from him? Do I want to be altered by him? Augmented? Improved? Undermined? Unaffected? It's hard to know what would be best for him, and for me. Perhaps it was wrong of me to give him a project – the Derrida thing – but then again I can't just say, 'Write!' and expect him to get on with it. Maybe I should speak to him and find out what he'd prefer. I sometimes wonder if this book seems real to him, and whether it's a pressure, a pleasure, or what. I know he works very hard and that finding time to write can't be easy. One temptation is to quietly write loads and fill up the pages myself in order to take the pressure off him. But would that be good hosting?

These worries all seem to circle around politeness, embarrassment, and how to conduct a worthwhile dialogue. Now that we're up and running, I see how naïve it was to imagine that two people who are immersed in very different discourses might be able to get together and make some kind of coherent pronouncement. It feels a bit like one of those dreams where you're driving a car but none of the controls are quite what or where they should be. I suppose I had the idea that being asked to write for publication is some kind of honour and that it was an inherently 'nice' thing to invite someone to do. But it's a lot of work, potentially uncomfortable and exposing, and there's not necessarily any tangible reward. Poor Robert! What on earth am I trying to achieve here with him? Are there things I can do to make this a good experience for him? The fact that he writes on a typewriter makes me think he prefers to keep our texts very separate. I suppose that's a big clue as to how he's approaching this collaboration, and it would seem wise to respect that. I think. As I bide my time waiting for his response, I'm realising there are other dynamics at play in our conversation – dynamics like embarrassment and politeness. Perhaps I need to look more closely at these phenomena to make more sense of the process of listening we are engaged in.

Politeness is a perennial problem for psychoanalysts: how do you get people to hear things they don't want to hear without offending them? In regular, daily life it's intrinsically rude to confront people with unpleasant information. So is the job to be rude to people, but in just the right way? Different schools have radically different ideas about how to go in with interpretations: being slow and waiting till the analysand basically already knows it, versus the shock tactic of confronting people in real time, as the matter presents itself. Clinical psychoanalysis is a place where the conventions around social interaction and conversation are slightly differently played out, but they're certainly not done away with.

From a certain perspective, the whole history of psycho-analytic technique could be framed as a question of how polite to be. You can't just say, 'Try to be tactful and beyond that, anything goes.' The various schools of analysis would tend to lean in drastically different directions with regard to how soon to interpret, how forcefully, and which material to emphasise. Do you have to present people with their pesky tendencies immediately and in every instance? For example, making someone feel bad about being late would be terrible social behaviour, but for many British analysts would be par for the course: 'You're expressing your hostility by making me wait.' While Lacanians don't do that, we might cut people off mid-flow and send them out onto the street. Or, following Bruce Fink's advice on Lacanian technique, we might set out by picking people up on every single linguistic idiosyncrasy; also a conversational no-no. And that's all before you get round to telling people that they seemed to enjoy listening to their parents having sex, or whatever. Basically, you could say that psychoanalysis just *is* deeply impolite. But do you deal with that by brazening out the rudeness, or do you develop crafty ways to mitigate it? How would you decide given the wide range of possibilities? There are the different theoretical orientations, but also your personal style, coupled with the impression you have of the person you're dealing with. Who are they? What can they take? In other words, it's a minefield.

If there's little in psychoanalytic theory to help us regulate our politeness levels, we could look to other disciplines. One helpful study comes from anthropological linguistics. In 1978, Penelope Brown and Stephen Levinson published 'Universals in Language Usage: Politeness Phenomena' – a very influential paper, even though there's plenty to take issue with in it. For example, they use three languages, or cultures, from which to extrapolate a universal theory, which is obviously mad.

To lay out the basic premises of their argument, Brown and Levinson put forward the idea that human interactions revolve around the idea of 'face', as in 'saving face'. (The idea of 'face' is central to Chinese culture although, according to LuMing Robert Mao, their theory is problematised if you try to apply it to typical Chinese social interactions. Oh well.) For Brown and Levinson, face has two aspects: negative and positive. Negative face involves being able to go about your business uninterrupted, to have the freedom to do the things you want to do, while positive face means being respected, and having your wants and desires supported by others. So a 'Model Person', or 'rational being', wants to sustain both negative and positive face as far as possible at all times. They want to be unimpeded in their wishes, and to be loved or admired for the things they do. To be fair on Brown and Levinson, they concede that this may not be the whole story where human beings are concerned, but they also argue that so much goes on in support of these aims you have to take them seriously. They don't deny the idea of a perverse unconscious: they're just dealing with the stuff you can see in daylight. (You could also argue that the unconscious part of politeness *is* hostility, so it's a perfect illustration of the notion that the unconscious hides itself in full view.)

Obviously, in order to function socially, Model People, or MPs, will either have to frustrate or enlist other MPs, which is where things start to get messy. Sometimes you may want to be free to do things that other people won't respect you for, or maybe other MPs want to encroach on your negative face in support of their face needs.

It's generally thought to be advantageous to have as many people's face needs being met at once, so everyone has to come up with variety of tricks for dealing with the inevitable affronts we both receive and dish out. All this perhaps resonates with the early Freudian idea that hate comes before love; that when you're born the entire world is basically an irritant and you have to find ways to deal with that. Politeness theory also has its roots in master/slave dialectics and the notion of conflicting subjectivities trying to work something out between themselves. However, instead of a straightforward battle for pure prestige you get a muddle of aggressive and defensive strategies, with different things seeming like good ideas at different times. When read from a psychoanalytic perspective it's funny as well as illuminating. The whole problem revolves around greed and aggression and how near-impossible it is for people to peacefully coexist. Still, Brown and Levinson are saying it in a polite way – it's a polite theory. It's not explicitly stated that you might want to fuck the people you're not supposed to fuck and to destroy your peers, although that's the implication. Freud might be rude enough to say all that, but Brown and Levinson are not. Instead, they focus on the details in language that give the game away.

The big thing you need to watch out for in human interaction is the 'Face Threatening Act'. Much, if not most, social exchange involves mitigating FTAs. An FTA could be anything from asking someone to pass the salt (interfering with their negative face) to pointing out in front of a court that the same person is a selfish, thieving sociopath (bad for positive face).

Brown and Levinson's study is totally obsessional, full of lists, sub-lists, and diagrams. It's also beautifully paranoiac in its claims that compliments and expressions of admiration are considered FTAs every bit as imposing as overt affronts. Brown and Levinson run through all the possible FTAs that threaten negative face, such as requests to do or not do things, suggestions, reminders, threats, offers, promises, and expressions of strong emotion – this last being particularly good as it puts saying 'I love you' and 'I want to punch you' in the same structural position. Then there are the threats to positive face, like criticism, ridicule, challenges to opinion, irreverence, bringing bad news about the person, blatant non-cooperation in an activity in which a person is invested, and misaddressing someone. Of course, these two sets of possibilities overlap because it's not uncommon for positive and negative face to be threatened simultaneously.

While these FTAs are relevant to the addressee, the speaker themselves may also threaten their own face by apologising, laughing, or crying inappropriately, acting stupid or confessing, expressing thanks, making excuses, accepting an offer, or noticing that the other person has committed a faux pas.

Here you end up with a very useful four-way grid system for classifying FTAs. But you also need to be aware of tactics for committing these FTAs in the first place. Everyone is constantly at risk – Brown and Levinson call it 'mutual vulnerability of face'. The options here are whether to commit the FTA on the record, off the record, or not at all, and whether to do it with or without redressive action. In other words, whether you should criticise someone to their face or behind their back, and whether, in either case, you should soften your critical assessment somehow, maybe by saying something nice about them too. An on-the-record FTA without redressive action might save face if it means people give you credit for honesty, whereas an off-the-record FTA might be seen as kinder. If you hate your friend's new partner, you could simply tell them outright, or you could discuss it with a mutual friend and keep it to yourselves. Then again, this might seem sneaky, so you'd have to think about how to mitigate that. Perhaps you could try something on the record but with redressive action, therefore appearing admirably diplomatic. You could perhaps say that you hadn't been quite sure whether you liked the person at first but that you could imagine becoming fonder of them in the future if you got to know them a little better. In short, you need to be aware of all face needs involved at any given moment and to be thinking constantly in terms of damage limitation.

Brown and Levinson's main focus is on linguistic constructions around FTAs, like putting loads of waffle before a request: 'I hate to bother you but I was wondering whether...' Ums and ahs are also good, as is shuffling around and looking meek. You can certainly combine non-linguistic strategies with linguistic ones. Good examples of non-linguistic tricks might be things like raised eyebrows or sending an emissary – maybe getting your friend to tell someone you fancy them so they don't have to feel so pained about rejecting you. There are also more subtle ways of getting your obnoxious requests past people, like using the first-person plural, as in 'Give us a smile' or 'lend us a tenner', suggesting it's not just your own good you're thinking of.

From this perspective, all social existence is a kind of infinite, inverse fight in which we are fighting against fighting all the time. The study goes on to show how the same tricks work in parts of Mexico and India (just don't try it in China).

What might all this mean in the consulting room? In the battles over the regulation of therapy in the UK, there was talk of standardising, and insisting on, certain behaviours such as handshaking to greet patients. Some people thought that shaking your patient's hand on the way in and out was a good idea, while for most psychoanalysts it would be nuts to adhere to a ritual of demonstrating that you're not carrying a weapon. If you want to unnerve someone, maybe make a big song and dance about how harmless you are. Niceties like asking people how they are – or answering when they ask you – are all done away with in analytic practice. If people insist on saying apparently insignificant stuff on the way in and out of sessions you have to take what they say as serious fodder for analysis. Maybe they are trying to find something out about you while you are off-guard. Perhaps they can't tolerate silence. Maybe they feel they have to give something back after all the attention you have given them. But will you be rude and ask outright what the hell they think they're doing? Or will you wait until they've worked it out for themselves?

On the analyst's side, politeness probably cannot be managed by shuffling around and adding loads of qualifiers before you make an intervention. That would only lead to embarrassment on both sides. But perhaps there is a place for embarrassment in even the best managed of dialogues.

In the first sentence of Oliver T. Dann's 'A Case Study of Embarrassment' (1977), he tells us that 'embarrassment has been largely overlooked as a subject for psychoanalytic study' before going on to cite about forty articles dealing with the subject, not to mention outlining Freud's super-famous theory of embarrassment from *The Interpretation of Dreams*. (I feel bad about the fact that I'm trying to embarrass Oliver Dann when he's not around to defend himself. I'm also aware that trying to embarrass other people is very poor social behaviour and that the person who deserves to feel embarrassed about it is me. Look at me mitigating my FTA like a pro!)

We might as well lay Freud's theory out at the start because, in a sense, it's the psychoanalytic bottom line with regard to embarrassment and enjoyment. His section on 'Typical Dreams' begins with 'The embarrassment-dream of being naked'. Freud explains that this seemingly universal dream is born from the pleasure of exposing oneself in front of one's parents as a child. The embarrassment is an effect of repressed exhibitionism. It's Freud 101 in that everything's the opposite of the way it initially appears: parents are represented by strangers, pleasure is registered as displeasure, and so on. It's a beautiful theory, with an unmistakeable aura of truth, and it means psychoanalysts tend to slap a pleasure label on anything that claims to be painfully embarrassing. 'You say it's embarrassing but you love it! Your unconscious has got one over on you, and at least a part of you is having a really good time!'

In psychoanalytic literature, you will find everything from the idea that not nearly enough has been said about embarrassment to the idea that there may not be that much to say in the first place, because it's pretty easy to understand, to the idea that the whole of psychoanalysis is basically a theory and practice of embarrassment. In Oliver Dann's two-page literature review you could even be left with the impression that psychoanalysis is nothing more than a pure experience of embarrassment. We read that people come to us to talk about things they'd be too embarrassed to say to other people, that they do it on a couch because it would be embarrassing to look us in the face while they're saying it. It might also be embarrassing for us to be seen to hear it, according to Frieda Fromm-Reichmann: another good argument for use of the couch. Kurt R. Eissler had the opposing idea that psychoanalysts are generally supposed not to suffer from embarrassment – we've been cured of it in our training analyses – although Lucia Tower, in an essay from 1956, felt she had noticed a good deal of embarrassment in people's writings concerning countertransference (the analyst's feelings about the patient), especially when something of it has slipped out in a session. Leon Saul (1966) tells us over and over again that nakedness dreams can be related to transference: something embarrassing comes out in analysis and then the analysand has a nakedness dream.

Then there's the untangling, or not, of embarrassment and shame, and shame and guilt. In *The Interpretation of Dreams*, Freud uses various terms seemingly interchangeably, while contemporaries such as Sándor Ferenczi and Theodor Reik use several German words which have been bundled together by English translators under the term 'embarrassment'. For example, you might argue that Ferenczi's ideas about embarrassment, scopophilia, exhibitionism, and masturbation might be better understood using the word shame.

But what's the difference between shame and embarrassment? For some it's simply a matter of degree – embarrassment is like diet shame. For others it has more to do with the place of the observer – you can't feel embarrassment if no one's witnessed your embarrassing act, but you can feel shame about something no one else knows about. Shame relies more heavily on intrapsychic mechanisms, although both involve falling short of an ideal. Then there's guilt, and the moral failure it involves, although you may feel guilty about falling short of an ideal that you don't actually believe in. Perhaps you feel guilty about not being the person your parents want you to be, at the same time as having no interest in actually being that person.

Embarrassment could also be understood as a defence against shame – if something causes you to experience shame, it might send you to work a bit more, but if you can keep it at the level of embarrassment you don't have to deal with it quite so urgently. (This is the thrust of of Helen Lynd's work on shame and identity from 1958.) More recently, there's plenty of material about shame in Adam Phillips's book *Attention Seeking* (2019). There's abundant scope for embarrassment in this area as most of us have been socialised, or semi-socialised, out of attention seeking and therefore find it deeply shameful, or at least embarrassing, to be caught at it – especially if we fail to impress or make people like us in the process. In short, attention seeking can be catastrophic for our own positive face, and potentially for the negative face of others too. Phillips has the idea that your style, or character, comes out of your particular mode of shame, and that most of us are liable to exist in a shameful relationship to love, money, sex, food, fame, or politics.

Embarrassment may also be part of a wider problem of 'social anxiety'. Otto Fenichel wrote about this as early as the 1940s. He mentions embarrassment being ramped up into a symptom like erythrophobia – a fear of blushing – which might be understood in terms of a ferocious superego, or an over-investment in other people's thoughts and opinions, or both. Fenichel speaks about erythrophobia alongside stage-fright and the notion that overtly exhibitionistic behaviours might result in some form of castration or loss of love. Performing in front of people is intrinsically risky, and glossophobia, the fear of public speaking, according to the National Institute of Mental Health in America, affects around 73% of people, ranking as the fourth most common phobia after fear of death, spiders, and heights. (Fear of death is counted as a phobia?!)

According to Fenichel, people who perform in front of others are liable to develop quite desperate tricks in order to defend themselves against the horror of the activity they're engaged in. Maybe they are compelled to cause people to laugh or clap in order to demonstrate that there are no hard feelings. He writes:

> The idea is by magical gestures to force spectators to prove that no castration has occurred, or to give the approbation needed to contradict a guilt feeling; if the spectators do not fulfil these demands immediately and adequately, violent (oral) sadistic tendencies may be developed against them.

It's curious that the grammar is unclear here – it could either be the audience or the guilt feelings that suddenly find themselves under attack. The paragraph actually goes on to make it clear that the violence is liable to be turned inward. As he puts it, 'What is done to protect the person's self-esteem against danger may result in the opposite, in his complete annihilation.' In other words, he alludes to the experience that stand-up comedians describe as 'dying'. Fenichel has a succinct description of the familiar-seeming subject position with regard to performing: 'The [person] believes unconsciously that he is castrated and fears that his attempts to deny it might fail, and that everything that was intended to make people like and feed him might result in their disliking him and withdrawing all support.'

From this psychoanalytic literature on embarrassment, some but not all of it kindly provided by Oliver Dann, psychoanalysis emerges thoroughly infused with embarrassment and could even be said to be built entirely from it. We are faced with so many ways of thinking about embarrassment it's hard to know where to look, although you could say there's a loose division between seeing it as a social effect – an effect of being overly interested in what goes on in other people's minds – and seeing it as something self-involved and masturbatory; a phantasy that comes with a set of physical sensations. However, as psychoanalysts often seem to agree, those sorts of binaries aren't really viable. Perhaps the thing about embarrassment is that it's emphatically both.

All of this echoes some of the questions that circulate around Lacan's concept of jouissance (a kind of problematic, painful enjoyment). There's the supposedly asocial, autoerotic aspect of a person's modes of enjoyment, but also potentially an appeal to the Other, even in the most seemingly furtive forms of troubled enjoyment. Embarrassment, too, is both inward- and outward-looking. It can be intensely bodily while simultaneously being a kind of out-of-body experience, where the minds of others are felt somehow to have power over your being. If they've clocked this *thing* about you, they will think badly of you, and you might fear you're unable to bear that.

Stepping away from the psychoanalytic literature, one of the most amazing chroniclers of embarrassment is the sociologist Erving Goffman. In 'Embarrassment and Social Organisation' (1956) Goffman comes at things from social psychology, observing the signs of embarrassment from the outside, and attempting to understand them in relation to social systems. His essay contains excruciatingly observed accounts of embarrassment, beginning with a list of possibilities:

> An individual may recognise extreme embarrassment in others, and even in himself, by the objective signs of emotional disturbance: blushing, fumbling, stuttering, an unusually low or high pitched voice,

quavering speech or breaking of the voice, sweating, blanching, blinking, tremor of the hand, hesitating or vacillating movement, absent-mindedness and malapropisms. [...] There are also symptoms of a subjective kind: constriction of the diaphragm, a feeling of wobbliness, consciousness of strained and unnatural gestures, a dazed sensation, dryness of the mouth, and tenseness of the muscles.

So, there are a huge number of ways in which embarrassment might manifest itself. Goffman goes on to say, 'In the popular view, it is only natural to be at ease during interaction, embarrassment being a regrettable deviation from the normal state.' If you show signs of embarrassment, it appears that something is going wrong, or shouldn't be happening in the way it's happening. He calls all these phenomena 'the flustering syndrome'. If you experience them too often, too intensely, or too visibly, you might be 'regarded as suffering from a foolish, unjustified sense of inferiority and in need of therapy'.

Goffman talks about the way in which *any* human interaction has the capacity to become embarrassing to one or more participants, or even for everyone involved. He does make special mention of 'pairs of participants who are together having difficulties', which perhaps brings to mind much reality TV – particularly, perhaps *Love Island* – where the management of embarrassment has been turned into a competitive sport, and where being a bit embarrassed can be much more winning than not being embarrassed enough. Time is also an important element in the experience of embarrassment; there are slow-burn, long-lasting embarrassments – perhaps about your college grades, or general inability to make it through a feature film without needing to pee – and more intense outbursts, perhaps caused by a public gaffe. As Goffman tells us, 'Some occasions of embarrassment seem to have an abrupt, orgasmic character.' Still, he doesn't seem to be saying that the embarrassment is, in itself, enjoyable – more that something bad has marred a euphoric moment and that the euphoria has become momentarily mixed in with the badness. For Goffman, embarrassment is largely seen as something to be avoided, although it's apparently endearing when people are thrown off-guard by compliments. If you can't avoid embarrassment, the thing to do is to pretend it isn't happening. He says, 'To appear flustered in our society [...] is considered evidence of weakness, inferiority, low-status, moral guilt, defeat, and other unenviable attributes.' Therefore people develop all sorts of techniques for concealing this state – as the seventeenth century wit Lord Chesterfield puts it, 'a thousand tricks to keep themselves in countenance' – rubbing their noses, scratching their heads, or twirling their hats. Anything to give you something to do with your body while you get your unfortunate feelings back in check. According to Goffman, these fiddly gestures are screens to hide behind while you work out what to do, and different people will be differently good at dissembling. He mentions public speaking: you might get some of the awkward phenomena sorted – your voice stops quavering and you start thinking you're pretty cool – but the people sitting next to you can see that your hands are shaking.

It would be extremely rude of observers to let you know they can see how nervous you are – because embarrassment is, at bottom, an admission of failure – so one of the secondary effects of embarrassment is that it sends other people to work, trying to pretend they haven't noticed. Goffman gives a brilliant description of the intersubjective experience of embarrassment when one person is desperately trying to conceal their loss of composure and the other is frantically trying to demonstrate that they haven't noticed. There's the risk of an embarrassment feedback loop where both sides fail to annul the embarrassment, which escalates until it would be impossible and even more embarrassing to ignore, until it finally announces itself fully in some kind of terrible eruption – someone collapses into tears of laughter, 'has a temper tantrum, flies into a blind rage, faints,

dashes to the nearest exit, or becomes rigidly immo-
bile [...] In short, he abdicates his role as someone who
sustains encounters.' (Note here that Goffman provides
a good description of a psychoanalyst – someone who
sustains encounters. It would be extremely unnerving
if they were so unable to deal with embarrassment that
they became rigid or ran out of the room.)

How does a person become able to deal with embarrassment? Kurt R. Eissler might have the idea that you
can be psychoanalysed out of it, and Saul suggests that
you might work it through in your transference dreams,
but those are not the only options. Goffman states that
teasing, even a bit of bullying, is a method for training
people to hold their poise. You have to learn to keep
your composure while being insulted, having your faults
pointed out, and noticeably losing at games. Sports like
cricket specifically encourage people to stay stylish
under duress, which is why it's taught in English public
schools: how will you ever be prime minister if you can't
pretend everything's OK when it isn't? Perhaps we can
at least agree that this is a more embarrassing job than
being a psychoanalyst...and that Freud's 'impossible
professions' – educating, healing, governing – are also
the embarrassing ones. (Pedagogy is obviously very embarrassing – ask any academic.)

Anyhow, it's of the utmost importance for everyone, not
just psychoanalysts, professors, and prime ministers, to
learn to manage their embarrassment, at least according
to Goffman in 1950s America. Being difficult to embarrass
is a social duty. Your lack of embarrassment reassures
other people that everything is OK.

In psychoanalytic dialogue, though, as opposed to a
Goffman-style American barbecue or business meeting,
there might be something like an invitation to embarrassment. There might or might not be a space to say something of what you really think or want, rather than what
you are comfortable with thinking you want; an invitation

to sustain a different sort of encounter where the rules of engagement are less proscribed, which might lead to embarrassment, but possibly also enjoyment, although this enjoyment would surely be unstraightforward and infused with anxiety or some other bothersome affect. It's the sort of destabilising, potentially anxiety-provoking dialogue that might not suit everyone.

Not all of the gods are good at listening. Supplications
offered up to the likes of Bacchus, Baal or Yahweh resemble
one clutching at the feet of a pissed off partner and
delivering a cry for release from the irrational agony of a
 relationship. The assymetry that asks for oxen and other
torn forms of sacrificial tissue does not require the devotee
to have a voice or dare to ask for dialogue. One could
imagine being broken at the altar if asking to be heard by
the god instead of mutely obeying and putting a torch to
the flesh-crested pyre.

The begging human chorus is here curtailed in smoke that
will reach the nostrils of the gods if the best bits of a
body are burned. It is one version of a conversation with
 the Divine, in which listening, at least on their side,
plays no part.

But this never stops us from asking to be heard. So we
 carve new faces for a flux of refashioned Absolutes with
actual ears. Krishna cries tears of milk and Christ draws
in the dirt while inclining his head, so we know they are
listening. This allows us to turn fragrant smoke into
entreaties and ash into words. Charred flesh is swapped out
for flowers, pitiless log piling and smoking slaughter for
something called prayer, another approach to a silent parent
 with perhaps enough music in the lines to get them to listen.

"I pray to God to rid me of God."

Here is my query: In Eckhart's great ask, was he seeking
the un-nameable, beyond human concepts and monikers? Was
he tearing down the idols he made to the "I AM" from the
cold stone of language and the frustrated imagination?
Or was he being straightforward and sincere, asking the
divine silence to rid him of the unhearing Emptiness.

And he penned his prayer:
He penned his prayer, writing to whom?

In the candlelit quiet of his cell, is Meister Eckhart
beseeching the deity or calling out to a real human reader
in another room, and asking her to listen.

"God is dead... and we have killed them... must we not become
gods simply to be worthy of the deed?"

What kind of god would Nietzsche have his new human become?
An on-the-march Ubermensch in Dionysian overdrive is one
obvious answer; an artist in their better garb choosing the
foxtrot over the goose-step, a conductor (musical mosh pits
 - not trams) of a solitary opera...

Can we take up his call to be "worthy of the deed" and do
more than become wannabe Brancusi's, sculpting deiform
masks to use on parade? In piercing the wax-filled ears of
the immortals and, beginning to listen, can we be unbound
from the gods, unseat our avatars, bypass the desire to
become a deaf demiurge and fashion ourselves into a friend?

When trying to decide whether to take someone on for psychoanalysis there are two key things to think about: them and you. Is it likely to be a good idea for them? And for you? And how much can you know about either in advance? For guidance, there's always Freud's entertaining and helpful paper, 'On Psychotherapy' (1905), in which he has some pretty directive ideas.

'On Psychotherapy' is one of those essays where Freud's at his most normcore. He's discussing the actual work of psychotherapy – trying to make people feel better – as opposed to simply trying to elaborate psychoanalytic theory. It's clear that the two enterprises intersect but aren't the same, and also that other things, like organic medicine, might just as well intersect with psychotherapy; you may think you're being a surgeon or a haematologist, but actually you're being used as a therapist by your patients whether you like it or not. Because of this, as a psychoanalyst, you might as well take the therapy side of your work seriously and try to know whatever you can know about it. People can sometimes come over quite hard-line about psychoanalysis not being there to make people feel better. However, while it might not aim at quick symptom removal, it doesn't follow that one isn't bothered about the suffering of one's patients. Here Freud says something funny. He's obliged to put an emphasis on psychoanalysis proper – as opposed to distraction, suggestion, and exercise – because it's his pet project. Still, that doesn't stop him regularly telling people, '"Don't worry, you'll soon be alright again" [...] our usual words of comfort which we dispense so liberally to our patients.'

Freud concedes that psychoanalysis isn't for everyone. So who is it *not* for? He draws up a list of four contraindications, or reasons not to treat someone:

> 1.'[T]hose patients who do not possess a reasonable degree of education and a fairly reliable character.'

Of course, no contemporary practitioner is likely to stand by this. People without formal educations regularly make the most amazing analysands and are often better able than snotty intellectuals to make the best of the analytic set-up. Also, 'fairly reliable' is a description so loose and psychoanalytically untenable as to be happily ignored.

Freud also warns that 'There are healthy people as well as unhealthy ones who are good for nothing in life,' and we should steer clear of these. The problem is that they can be hard to spot, and anyhow their worthiness or unworthiness can only ever be a matter of opinion. He adds to these people who have been sent to analysis by their relatives. These aren't a definite no-no, but apparently you'd better look into it. Is it that they are being sent reluctantly, or that they like spending their relatives' money? In either case it could be a problem.

In playing off and problematising the two possibilities of 'therapy' and 'psychoanalysis', Freud uses the word 'educable' (*erziehbar*) a number of times, but what he means by 'educable' seems to be something quite complex. It might not mean a capacity to improve by general social standards, but to be able to bear something difficult.

> 2. 'Psychoses, states of confusion and deeply rooted [..] depression are [...] not suitable for psychoanalysis.'

Freud does however mention a possible future in which developments in technique make it possible to work with psychotics – and obviously that's where the post-Freudian schools of analysis have come up with various possibilities which could generally be categorised as 'be kind and definitely don't do classical psychoanalysis on them'.

3. 'Old people are no longer educable.'

People over the age of fifty lack mental elasticity, according to Freud, which is notable as he was forty-nine at the time of writing.

4. 'Psychoanalysis should not be attempted where the speedy removal of dangerous symptoms is required.'

Treating severe anorexia through analysis, for instance, would be a bad idea because the person might die of malnutrition before the analysis started to work on them.

These are all reasons to say 'no' that come from the patient's side, but we're obviously talking about a two-way street. Freud reminds us that, thanks to repression and resistance, you should be prepared to 'expect unpleasantness of various kinds'. He states that psychoanalysis makes huge demands on both patient and analyst. For the patient, it demands radical honesty, plus it takes time and money. For the analyst, it also takes time and involves a big, difficult training, not to mention ongoing patience and tolerance of discomfiting transferential effects – primarily being loved and hated. It's in this essay that Freud says psychoanalysis was invented for 'patients permanently unfit for existence' and that if you genuinely think the person could be helped by easier, quicker means you should encourage them towards that.

Jump forward a hundred years and some other perspectives are provided in a 2003 study from the *Scandinavian Psychoanalytic Review*, 'Which patients should avoid psychoanalysis, and which professionals should avoid psychoanalytic training? A critical evaluation'. In spite of the swashbuckling title, it turns out to be a kind of quick-sand essay – all definite ideas get swiftly sucked back under. It states upfront that it's going to be evidence-based and thoroughly sensible, while conceding that psychoanalysis doesn't really work like that – and then goes onto demonstrate why not.

The author, Sverre Varvin, presents a view of an analytic world that's very much in a state of change and flux. It's nice because it doesn't even hint at conflict but draws a picture of all the different schools – 'Kleinian, self-psycho-logy, object-relational, interpersonal, Lacanian' – all in a 'process of development and [...] characterised by mutual influence and internal change'. This idealised misrep-resentation suggests Scandinavians are extremely civ-ilised. The study points out that many of these schools have found their identities in a capacity to treat patients deemed unsuitable for analysis.

The main contraindication in the case of classical psycho-analysis, for example, is severe psychopathology, as the patient's ego isn't strong-yet-flexible in quite the right way to bear the difficulties of standard analytic tech-nique. As Bernard Apfelbaum has joked, post-Freudians are often 'more concerned with how not to do analysis than with how to do it'. Freud faced the problem of whether to change his approach or to refuse patients who couldn't take it. The question remained unresolved, although mid-century Freudians perhaps became a bit too keen on the latter. Since the 1950s we have had Lacan's ideas about how to treat psychotic patients (be-come a 'secretary to the insane') and more recently the French psychoanalytic notion of 'mentalisation' to treat people with severe personality disorders, popularised by Peter Fonagy since the 1990s (remind them that oth-er people's internal realities are as real as their own). These days, according to Apfelbaum, 'Lack of reflective capacity is no longer a contraindication.' Yay! Now we can work with as many sociopaths as we like.

The Scandinavian study heavily cites a book by Ralph R. Greenson from 1974, *The Technique and Practice of Psychoanalysis*, which puts forward two questions: is the patient analysable, and is psychoanalysis the treatment most likely to help them? Greenson agrees with many others in the field in saying that suffering and curiosity about one's suffering are essential, as well as an idea that one's suffering is bound up with one's personality or character formation. But he also has a list of Romeo and Juliet-like pairs of antithetical ego functions that make for a good analysand: 'To be able to regress and progress, be passive and active, give up control and maintain control, and both renounce and retain reality testing'. The patient should also be able to sustain a complex transference alongside a good working alliance; to understand that if they love or hate you that's just a feature of the work. They also need to demonstrate a certain level of impulse control so that they can contain themselves after sessions where a lot of uncomfortable material has come out, or where they've regressed.

Some later research from the 1980s, by Irwin Hirsch, moves away from the idea of the 'good patient' and starts to look at the two-sidedness of the analytic relationship. For Hirsch, analysability is 'also a function of the analyst's personality, personal myths, theoretical orientation', etc. Instead of asking whether people are analysable, you might start asking who they could be analysed by. To quote Varvin, 'We must not only ask which patients should avoid psychoanalysis, but also which patients should avoid analysis with which analysts under which circumstances.' For example, I learnt in my twenties that I should avoid object-relations analysts as their emphasis on my distress around their absences (due to holidays, for example) really pissed me off. I double checked in 2014 and it was still true. However, my main reproach against my parents is that they went on a long holiday that entailed their missing my first birthday, so the problem with object relations therapy is undeniably, in part, on my side. I agree with much of their theory but their technique is intolerable. I know this has everything to do with me, and you could say I should work through it with one of them – in fact some of them have said that, rather forcefully – but I would say thank goodness for Lacanian psychoanalysis. However, it's not just theoretical orientation that makes the difference. It's also how the individual therapist works. I still hold out the fantasy of my perfect Kleinian who could actually 'cure' me in the way they seem to promise.

Greenson talks about qualities like 'compassion, concern and warmth which are not traditionally associated with "classical psychoanalysis"' but which might be embodied by a practitioner of any theoretical bent. In terms of who is or isn't analysable, if you get a practitioner who is able to combine softer, supportive qualities with sharp analysis – and to be flexible with different patients about which facets of the work to emphasise – then you probably go some way towards explaining the phenomenon of 'super-therapists', which you often read about in more recent studies of the efficacy of talking cures. If people are clever about balancing the hard stuff with the soft stuff, they're almost certainly going to work better with more patients than people who get stuck being either too 'nice' or too 'nasty' and can therefore only work with patients who happen to be compatible with their particular distortion. In short, you might say a good analyst, like a good dominatrix, is someone who knows how to combine warmth and compassion with frustration and pain.

Narcissists and masochists often get flagged up as kinds of people who may be unsuitable for analysis, but you could argue that the soft-soapers might often work quite sustainably with the narcissists, while the silent, tough cookies might find their match in the masochists. How much good they do in either case is up for discussion, but I like to adhere to the notion that each analyst gets the analysands they deserve.

These are some of the things that might be at stake when people talk to each other – especially in instances where there is an expectation that speaking will somehow make a difference. But alongside all the micro-instances of greater or lesser tact, mumbling versus precise interventions, silences, nods, witty ripostes, and the rest, we may have left aside a whole swathe of equally important phenomena, such as whether you can bear the other person enough to be there at all, let alone turn up for them week after week. While the craft of dialogue might be knotty and full of possibilities, perhaps the brute fact of demonstrating that you can tolerate the other person's being is as significant, if not more, than anything that can be put into words.

I'm still haunted by the words of the Indigenous elders: 'Why do people not listen when it's their own lives that are at stake?' I'm glad I was there to hear it, even if I still have no idea what I'm supposed to do. Listening is difficult and there are so many reasons not to do it.

Why do I still seem to want to insist on extracting words from Robert? Is it just for the sake of convention? Co-authored books are meant to be co-authored, after all. But what if his contribution is precisely *not* to write too much; to use his silence to cause me to say something? I can't work it out, but it might not be something I can work out on my own. Maybe the only thing for it is to speak to him.

Mill Road Cemetery

19 Dec 2021 44:20

00:01   00:02   00:03   00:04

00:02.59

RBY: Look, the phone knows where we are – speaking of listening.

AG: Oh my goodness, that's creepy. Shall I start with a sample question?

RBY: Yes please.

AG: Okay. I was curious about something in the letter you sent. You described something really material in the kind of listening you do. It seemed so different from the kind of listening I do. What you're listening out for is really something *else*. Still, there's supposedly this focus in my work on the materiality of language. It's not just about semantics – we're not simply looking for meaning in the things people say to us. It might be something in the phonemes that will tip you off to listen in a different way. Maybe some words rhyme or stick out because they're being used oddly. So, I wondered about this material, non-verbal listening that you seemed to be describing, and how you came to do that. What is possible to say about it?

RBY: I love that idea of materiality. You're dealing with gut wrapped in silver, with hair being pulled across it. That's what's creating the sound you're listening to. There's something within that sound that you're listening for as a maker, as you look to improve or adjust or shift it in some way or another. There's a very material element that has to do with the organic components, and within that, there's a vocabulary, developed by my colleague. He uses it very effectively, but it is completely inaccessible to me because I feel like I haven't learned it.

AG: Is it learnable?

RBY: Maybe. He describes things in terms of vowel sounds, and he'll hear something that's an 'aaaa' or 'eeee'. The question is what sounds more appealing when you're working with a certain combination of material elements.

AG: Is there consensus around what's appealing?

RBY: The way he transmits it, absolutely.

AG: Right.

RBY: It makes sense, and I agree with him. But when I've tried on my own to use that language or those tools, it's been ineffective. I feel like it remains inaccessible to me for now. But I have an aspiration to learn to listen and to describe sound in a similar way.

The vocabulary that I would tend towards has more to do with taste and sensation of acidity or sweetness or roundness in the mouth. Maybe it has more to do with bodily sensation, whereas his is more aural and, in some ways, more appropriate. But it's interesting to shift vocabularies, or personal vocabularies.

AG: So you developed your own vocabulary?

RBY: I think a lot of it is an act of ongoing plagiarism. People describe things that resonate and make sense and are catchy in a way that corresponds to their experience of hearing a note.

AG: Do musicians come with their own idiosyncratic vocabularies that you then have to interpret?

RBY: Yeah. Almost always. And sometimes it's unthinkingly inherited from a teacher or a mentor. I feel at times my task is to get them to use their own voice to describe their own experience of sound, without relying on what

I offer, or, more significantly, what's been offered or imposed by their mentors and teachers.

AG: And do they have very different ideas of – I don't know – would you call it beauty? Is the desired sound particular to each player?

RBY: It depends on the aspirations and the influences or pressures, many of them very much based on who they're working and playing for. There's immense variation. In some cases, it's a kind of monochrome aspiration towards a type of sound that can be heard at the back of a hall when you're screaming over an orchestra.

So, yes, there's a play between remarkable individuality, personal expression, variation, nuance, and interpretation, and then the cult of the soloist, which makes certain demands: being able to play a concerto, and to be heard, acknowledged, respected, and advanced. For me, there's a huge tension between the cult of the soloist and the sense of real listening for one's own potential voice.

When you hear Heifetz play, or when you hear a recording of Kreisler, Szigeti, some of earlier violinists, you know immediately who it is.

AG: What are the signs that tell you?

RBY: How much vibrato they use. Precision. The ability to work with mistakes. Allowing for them and dancing through them, especially in live recordings. An amount of grit, clarity, and speed. In certain players today there's something similar happening, which is wonderful. But I find a tragedy in the push to be able to play Sibelius, yet again, in front of a concert hall.

The reaction to that for many is doing period performance, which is an exciting arena.

AG: Trying to recreate the sound of a certain period?

RBY: Yeah. It is a wonderful world of exploration, like chamber music, that diminishes the soloist cult in a way I think it's important to do.

AG: I've got a question developing that's got so many parts that I don't think I'm going to be able to ask it... In psychoanalysis, you're always asking, 'what does this person want?' And I suppose you're problematising their speech and thinking, 'Whatever this person's telling me isn't necessarily what they're *actually* telling me.' So if they're telling you something else, then how do you listen for *that*? Maybe they're making a demand on you that's not explicit. How do you listen for other things? And are those other things always linguistic other things, or are they *other* other things?

RBY: I'm trying to relate that to the domain in which I function. When a violinmaker hears someone describing a sound they're looking for, they might wonder whether it is because it's something at a secondary level of interest, which may be their true interest, and may relate more to a particular voice that's important for that individual as an artist. The very simple, material, mechanical role that I would play in that is just trying to make an instrument a better tool for communicating that secondary layer.

Some of the first layers are pretty obvious or more easily communicable. More power and more projection, more colour and more depth. But there's a sense of nuance; maybe what happens when you play pianissimo. What is it in the playing that they're trying to draw forth? And why? And how does that relate to their experience of music and their longing within it?

AG: Yes.

RBY: If we listen for that, perhaps we can effectively move the sound or 'soul' of an instrument in a way that will augment a particular aspect of voice. Does a musician hear themselves better? Is it my role to even think that I can do that?

AG: Mm-hm.

RBY: Or is that exactly what we're meant to be doing, as mechanics – serving these people and just sharpening their tools? Or hoping to. It's so fucking satisfying when it works, and so often it's so minor. All you're doing is helping someone straighten the shoulders of their instrument, so everything is supported and lined up. Suddenly they have a voice that they didn't have five minutes before.

AG: So there's a cure element that's maybe similar to my work. If you can hear it right, then the instrument will be cured and the player will be able to play.

RBY: I wonder if it's cure, or just creating a larger stage to walk around and speak from.

AG: Right.

RBY: My question is, what does a musician listen for? What are they longing for? And how am I supposed to participate?

AG: To me your work seems like it's really at the limits of comprehensibility. The kind of listening you do is totally out there. Much more so than mine.

RBY: It's so subjective, and dependent on space and the qualities of a room. Whether there is or isn't a carpet on the floor, for instance, that makes a massive difference. [*phone rings*]

AG: Oh, do you want to answer it?

RBY: No. So, all of these things make a huge difference to the experience. But the subjectivity of it all, and the level of influence that someone in the mechanic's role can have, even momentarily, is disturbing to me. You know, people can be overconfident: 'Oh, now you're going to sound amazing because we've done this.'

AG: Oh yeah, that's like a chiropractor I saw.

RBY: Exactly. Like an overconfident chiropractor.

AG: That's terrible. Do some musicians experience a lot of anxiety in that moment of their instruments being moved around slightly?

RBY: Immense anxiety. I'm really interested in this intense, radical subjectivity in sound, and how dependent it is on someone's mood, and their anxiety levels. And the violinmaker who may be super nervous...

AG: Mm-hm.

RBY: ... because this is someone who's about to go on stage. There's a level of interdependence that can be magnificent and exciting, and so terrorising at the same time.

In the other half of my mind, I would love to have something more objective. I love to set up scientific rigs, for example, where you can do acoustic analysis that measures exactly what's happening at specific frequencies, or see where you have a damping effect when an instrument actually cuts out and is therefore more controllable. Some of the really nasty dog-whistle ends of the acoustic spectrum. In instruments that are more appreciated, quite often what happens is that they're actually dampened quicker, which allows one to shut them up faster and to close down frequencies that are unappealing.

AG: Right.

RBY: Therefore the whole thing is more sculptural, and offers a level of sculptability that something wild and new and kind of untamed and strident doesn't necessarily afford. But being able to objectify that in some way; to make that more analysable from a distance so it doesn't matter whether you've got a carpet on the floor or not. To analyse the object in its own right and to have some hard, very exquisite scientific data on acoustic response and sound.

AG: Do you think that would help somehow with someone's anxiety? I imagine that if musicians get a sort of obsessional idea that something isn't quite right, they could really amplify that in their imagination, and it would be really, really difficult to respond.

RBY: Very difficult. Because it's possibly happening on a level that's irrelevant to the instrument.

AG: Right, yeah.

RBY: And a level that's irrelevant to their capacity to express themselves musically. I like the idea of creating some base-level complement to language through data analysis and looking at sine wave functions and tonal curves. Again, dampening responses are fascinating to look at, as are intensities of emission at certain frequencies.

AG: What do you see there when you look?

RBY: You see patterns in the instruments that people find magnificent. Many of them old and Italian. You see patterns related to those instruments, where people agree there's a kind of voice with a clarity and purity, and a sonorous, potentially piercing quality.

You can find patterns of possibility, I would say. And patterns of function. You can adjust things to some degree. If you see a certain type of pattern that might need to be augmented for the musician, you can perhaps enhance that by different strings, soundpost movements, different forms of attention, by changing the bridge.

AG: Does that have a bearing on something like madness? I think about that a lot at the moment. Something to do with music and madness and meaning – madness happening when meaning becomes problematised. That's basically what madness is: meaning becoming excessive or vanishing. If you have those material ways of measuring something about sound, then it would cut a potential madness. It would interrupt the free-floating idea that something's wrong, or that something should be different.

RBY: I think you can potentially, in a very minor way, mitigate that. But this in no way, in my opinion, provides a substitute for the delirious, consequential and invested imbalance of listening.

AG: So the crazy, subjective thing is the thing?

RBY: Yeah. It really is. Even if we agree, there's an element of subjectivity in our agreement that I think is delightfully unstable.

AG: The more I hear you talk about your work, the more I think it's not as dissimilar from mine as I'd imagined.

RBY: I love that.

AG: It's funny, because some psychoanalysts believe in objective reality. There's the idea of the 'reality principle'; that you're bringing the analysand round to agree with you about what constitutes reality. But Lacanians especially think you can't have that. They think it's just ridiculous; everybody fantasises 'reality' differently, so whose reality would you go with? It's quite a difficult way to work. The idea that there's a reality you can both refer to is quite comforting... apparently.

RBY: 'The idea that there is a reality you can refer to is quite comforting.' There's something in trying to create that with the tools of science that's aesthetically absurd.

AG: Exactly. What you're doing, it's a response, isn't it? A response to something – to what, I don't know. To the demands made on you by people?

RBY: Mm-hm.

AG: Your work is your response.

RBY: Well, yeah. I'm the head of a scientific research department.

AG: OK.

RBY: So I need to do some science, and provide objective tools for our experience of sound. Which immediately makes me laugh. Because I think, well, what is science? And I'm meant to impose that on someone's perception of music…

AG: Mm-hm.

RBY: … of listening to themselves, and listening to themselves through an instrument that functions in various ways that can be adjusted or manipulated or augmented by the intervention of an individual with certain supposedly mysterious technical skills.

AG: I see.

RBY: And complementing that with… I don't know why it makes me laugh. But I saw an antique dentistry stand. I thought, 'Oh, it's obvious. That's what I need to put all of my super high-end equipment on.'

AG: Yeah.

RBY: And in the lab you're just like, 'Where am I?' And it looks super steampunk. I want to get the *Matrix/Blade Runner* screen thing going on.

AG: Yeah. That sounds essential. But it's funny as well, because it seems more credible, I think, in your field, that you run up against the limits of science. It's a real demonstration of those limits.

RBY: Yes. That's interesting.

AG: Maybe in my work the idea of science can be sort of embarrassing for us as practitioners.

RBY: That's something to explore. The limits of science in various fields.

AG: Yes. I think you're coming across legitimate limits, or legitimately exposing them.

RBY: And finding within them some potential to open a way or avenue for hearing things together with someone else. Let's listen for this frequency, and see how it changes on this graph. And on the other hand, hoping within that to clear the field, in a way, of anything claiming to be definitive or objective.

AG: All the stuff about machine listening is really bothersome to me. Apparently lots of people like talking to AI and being responded to by it.

RBY: Really?

AG: Apparently so. Yes.

RBY: OK.

AG: But what could a machine listen for? What do machines miss, and what are they better at? Like me with my dodgy shoulder, bad moods, hormones. All those things sometimes make me bad at listening; machines aren't bothered by that. So, there are these terrible payoffs in both areas; the wrongness of AI and the wrongness of people.

RBY: And when you feel that you're making an intervention by asking a question or responding, or following what you imagine to be a thread, a lapsus, or whatever it may be, the sense that if you do this, there will be a result – how do you feel about that relation? Is there predictability, or objectivity?

AG: It's just horrifying. I suppose that's why case histories are such a weird part of the field. Because when something happens, you can only extract meaning from it post hoc. Or you can lie. You can say, 'Because I made this intervention, this happened, or that person did this.' Their pains fell away, or they had an argument with their mum. Therapists often talk about cause and effect. But what difference does it make when someone comes to speak to someone else? It must make a difference. I wouldn't be a psychoanalyst if I didn't think speaking made a difference. But what is that difference?

RBY: And I would ask, how do you listen for that difference?

AG: Is it that you clear a space for the possibility of that difference? You definitely can't designate in advance what the difference would be. The notion that you're supposed to have a plan, or you're supposed to be listening for something, or you're supposed to know what to do with what you hear, which I think in modern therapies is a really big thing – they teach you what to do if someone tells you this or that – it seems misguided or clumsy.

RBY: Right, right.

AG: But with psychoanalysis, you don't know what to do with what people tell you, and you don't know what they do with what you say to them. There's this real emphasis on the unknowability of what happens in the exchanges of speech. And also the idea that that might be preferable to thinking you know, or to there being a science, or a procedure, or any kind of predictable sequence of cause and effect.

RBY: Do you feel like that confrontation with the inapplicability of cause and effect requires, encourages, allows for, permits, or divines in you clearer, better, more appropriate, potentially empathetic, truthful listening?

AG: I must think that otherwise it would be intolerable to try to do that kind of work. That's the promise of it, I guess.

RBY: And can you describe the promise? Or say more about the promise, or the possibility of the promise.

AG: This is a stupidly autobiographical answer, I guess, but because I grew up with a mum and dad who were involved in journalism, there was a lot of stuff in the air at home about the functionality of speech. Especially with tabloid journalism – which my mum did. You've got to be able to say things quickly; meaning has to be transferred really fast. It has to be unequivocal and clear. There has to be no mess.

In my family it felt like that was also expected of speech between each other. But there seemed to me to be lots of phenomena that weren't easily coverable by that. So I loved the idea that there was a place where you could speak and where you didn't have to transmit meaning quickly or urgently. You could come back to things later, or things could be messy, or not make sense. There was something other than the quick and functional transfer of meaning. Just that in itself was such a relief. There didn't have to be any great interpretations. That was the salve; it was enough to know that speech didn't need to make sense.

RBY: And the element of time – I hear it being woven into that.

AG: Oh yeah, I suppose I liked it that people wouldn't abandon you if you didn't make sense. The attempt to try to keep someone there is probably what's behind so much speech. Like, what are people trying to do when they speak? Obviously they're not just trying to describe things.

RBY: And the relation in your work between listening and time?

AG: It must be to do with attention and love. I think this is very common, but I certainly had the idea that you'd be abandoned if you couldn't say things in a way that drew the other person in. If you were slow or boring you would lose the other person. If you wanted to keep their attention, your speech had to be attention-grabbing.

RBY: Wow.

AG: But in a way that the other person liked.

RBY: That's so screwed up.

AG: I think a lot of it goes on. I'm not particularly haranguing my family. Probably even most speech is just that.

RBY: Oh yeah?

AG: I loved that there could be other forms of speech. I suppose in analysis you're paying someone not to be entertained. It's this other format for exchanging words with people.

RBY: So then you have the economy of listening.

AG: Exactly. That's a horror. I feel sick. I did not want to talk about this. How did we start talking about it?

RBY: Not even the economy in relation to money.

AG: No. Yeah. Exactly.

RBY: Other forms of economy, of affection.

AG: Yeah.

RBY: Attention. Acknowledgement.

AG: Oh God, yeah. Suddenly I feel absolutely freezing. Good conversation to have in a graveyard!

RBY: It's good. I love it. What a process.

AG: Should we pause?

Chantal Akerman (dir.), *A Couch in New York* (PolyGram, 1996).

Bernard Apfelbaum, 'Analysing, not Psychoanalysing', *Ego Analytic Psychology* (2016) <https://egoanalysisessays.wordpress.com/2016/08/29analyzing-not-psychoanalyzing/>

W. R. Bion, 'Notes on Memory and Desire', *Psychoanalytic Forum* 2:3 (1967), 272–280.

Eduardo Bonilla-Silva, 'The Linguistics of Color Blind Racism: How to Talk Nasty about Blacks without Sounding "Racist"', *Critical Sociology* 28:1–2 (2002), 41–64.

Penelope Brown and Stephen Levinson, 'Universals in Language Usage: Politeness Phenomena', in E. Goody (ed.), *Questions and Politeness Strategies in Social Interaction* (Cambridge: Cambridge University Press, 1978).

Francis Ford Coppola (dir.), *The Conversation* (Paramount, 1974).

Oliver T. Dann, 'A Case Study of Embarrassment', *Journal of the American Psychoanalytic Association* 25:2 (1977), 453–470.

Jacques Derrida and Anne Dufourmantelle, *Of Hospitality: Anne Dufourmantelle invites Jacques Derrida to respond*, trans. by Rachel Bowlby (Stanford: Stanford University Press, 1996).

Robin Di Angelo, *White Fragility* (Boston: Beacon Press, 2018).

Fredrik Falkenström, Fredrik Granström & Rolf Holmqvist, 'Working alliance predicts psychotherapy outcome even while controlling for prior symptom improvement', *Psychotherapy Research* 24:2 (2014), 146–159.

Otto Fenichel, *The Psychoanalytic Theory of the Neuroses* (London: Routledge, 1996).

Sándor Ferenczi, 'The Elasticity of Psycho-Analytic Technique'(1928), in *Final Contributions to the Problems and Methods of Psychoanalysis*, trans. by Eric Mosbacher (London: Karnac 1994).

Bruce Fink, *A Clinical Introduction to Lacanian Psychoanalysis: Theory and Technique* (Cambridge, MA: Harvard University Press, 1999).

Sigmund Freud, 'On Psychotherapy' (1905), in *The Standard Edition of the Complete Psychological Works of Sigmund Freud Vol. 7*, trans. by James Strachey (London: Random House, 2001).

Sigmund Freud, 'Papers on Technique'(1911–15), in *The Standard Edition of the Complete Psychological Works of Sigmund Freud Vol. 12*, trans. by James Strachey (London: Vintage Classics, 2001).

Sigmund Freud, 'Psychoanalysis Terminable and Interminable', trans. by Joan Riviere, *International Journal of Psycho-Analysis*, 18 (1937), 373–405.

Sigmund Freud, 'Recommendations to Physicians Practising Psycho-Analysis' (1912), in *The Standard Edition of the Complete Psychological Works of Sigmund Freud Vol. 12* trans. by James Strachey (London: Vintage Classics, 2001).

Sigmund Freud, *The Interpretation of Dreams*, trans. by Joyce Crick (Oxford: Oxford University Press, 1999).

Erving Goffman, 'Embarrassment and Social Organisation', *American Journal of Sociology* 62:3 (1956), 264–271.

Ralph R. Greenson, *The Technique and Practice of Psychoanalysis Volume 1* (London: Routledge, 2016).

Irwin Hirsch, 'Toward a More Subjective View of Analyzability', *American Journal of Psychoanalysis* 44 (1984), 169–182.

Ernest Jones, *The Life and Work of Sigmund Freud* (New York: Basic Books, 1953).

Spike Jonze (dir.), *Her* (Annapurna Pictures, 2013).

Jacques Lacan, 'The Function and Field of Speech and Language in Psychoanalysis' (1953), *Écrits*, trans. by Bruce Fink (New York: Norton, 2006).

Helen Merell Lynd, *On Shame And The Search For Identity* (London: Routledge, 1999).

LuMing Robert Mao, 'Beyond politeness theory: "Face" revisited and renewed', *Journal of Pragmatics* 21:5 (1994), 451–486.

Mike Noon, 'Pointless Diversity Training: Unconscious Bias, New Racism and Agency.' *Work, Employment and Society* 32:1 (2018), 198–209.

Walter J. Ong, *Orality and Literacy: The Technologizing of the Word* (New York: Methuen, 1982).

Adam Phillips, *Attention Seeking* (London: Penguin, 2019).

Claudia Rankine, *Just Us: An American Conversation* (Minneapolis: Graywolf Press, 2020).

Theodor Reik, *Listening with The Third Ear*: *The Inner Experience of a Psychoanalyst* (New York: Farrar and Straus, 1948).

Saul Rosenzweig, 'Some Implicit Common Factors in Diverse Methods of Psychotherapy', *American Journal of Orthopsychiatry* 6:3 (1936), 412–415.

J. D. Safran & J. C. Muran, 'The resolution of ruptures in the therapeutic alliance', Journal of Consulting and Clinical Psychology, 64:3 (1996), 447–458.

Arthur Schopenhauer, *Parerga and Paralipomena. Short Philosophical Essays, Volume 1* (Cambridge: Cambridge University Press, 2014).

Sherry Turkle, *Alone Together* (New York: Basic Books, 2011).

Sverre Varvin, 'Which patients should avoid psychoanalysis, and which professionals should avoid psychoanalytic training? A critical evaluation', *The Scandinavian Psychoanalytic Review* 26:2 (2003), 109–122.

We nearly didn't have an acknowlededgments page because it seemed too difficult. What if one of us wanted
to thank someone the other hadn't met? But then again,
wouldn't it be terrible not to thank people just because
there wasn't a single voice with which to do it? Would we
have to have two separate sections? Hadn't we learned
anything about co-authoring?

So, we both agree that we would like to thank Jess Gough
at MACK for being the most encouraging and receptive
editor, Michael Mack for including us in this series,
Morgan Crowcroft-Brown, Louis Rogers, and everyone
else at MACK who has been involved in producing the
book. We would also like to thank Poppy Sebag-Monte-
fiore, Devorah Baum, Josh Appignanesi, Darian Leader,
Lindsay Watson, Susan Morris, Tracey Cahoon, Miriam
Newman, Ajay and Ninder Khandelwal, Cedar Lewisohn
and Patricia Ellis, Dora Hargatai and Toby Brown, Andrea
Arnold, Ren Brown-Martin, Peter and Roslyn Grose, Dot
Grose Forrester, Orphée Sophie Juno, Nico Jenkins,
Amelie Violet, Pierre Smets, Esme Dora, Lucien Jamey,
Edith Doron, Christopher Fynsk, Agnes Victoria, Elfin
Vogel, and everyone else whose conversation and
friendship make our lives worth living. If you help one
of us, you're helping both of us. We would also like to
thank each other.

Also from this series

Anouchka Grose & Robert Brewer Young
Uneasy Listening: Notes on Hearing and Being Heard

First edition published by MACK
© 2022 MACK for this edition
© 2022 Anouchka Grose & Robert Brewer Young for their texts

Designed by Morgan Crowcroft-Brown
Edited by Jess Gough & Louis Rogers
Printed in Germany

ISBN 978-1-913620-77-6
mackbooks.co.uk